WELCO

PROBABLY THE BEST JOKE BOOK IN THE WORLD! FOR KIDS

300+ SILLY JOKES FOR FUNNY KIDS!

WHY DID THE BROOM GET A PROMOTION?

Because it was sweeping the competition!

WHAT DO YOU CALL A FUNNY MOUNTAIN?

Hill-arious!

WHY CAN'T A LEOPARD HIDE?

Because it's always spotted!

WHAT DO YOU CALL A MEDIEVAL LAMP?

A knight light!

WHY DID THE TOILET PAPER ROLL DOWN THE HILL?

To get to the bottom!

WHY ARE SKELETONS SO CALM?

Because nothing can get under their skin!

WHY DID THE BICYCLE FALL OVER?

Because it was two-tired!

WHAT DOES A SPIDER BRIDE WEAR ON HER WEDDING DAY?

A webbing dress!

WHAT DO YOU CALL A VERY POPULAR MOOSE?

Famoose!

WHAT DO YOU CALL A TALENTED FISH?

A starfish!

KNOCK KNOCK...

KNOCK KNOCK.
WHO'S THERE?
COW SAYS.
COW SAYS WHO?
NO, SILLY! COW SAYS MOO!

KNOCK KNOCK.
WHO'S THERE?
LETTUCE.
LETTUCE WHO?
LETTUCE IN, IT'S COLD OUT HERE!

KNOCK KNOCK.
WHO'S THERE?
BOO.
BOO WHO?
DON'T CRY, IT'S JUST A JOKE!

KNOCK, KNOCK.
WHO'S THERE?
OWL.
OWL WHO?
OWL BE SEEING YOU LATER!

KNOCK, KNOCK.
WHO'S THERE?
GOPHER.
GOPHER WHO?
GOPHER A WALK, IT'S A NICE DAY!

HA HA HA

KNOCK, KNOCK.
WHO'S THERE?
ALPACA.
ALPACA WHO?
ALPACA SUITCASE, LET'S GO ON A TRIP!

KNOCK, KNOCK.
WHO'S THERE?
I DID APP.
I DID APP WHO?
WELL I HOPE YOU FLUSHED THE TOILET!

KNOCK, KNOCK.
WHO'S THERE?
TANK.
TANK WHO?
YOU'RE WELCOME!

KNOCK, KNOCK.
WHO'S THERE?
MUSTACHE.
MUSTACHE WHO?
I MUSTACHE YOU A QUESTION, BUT I'LL SHAVE IT FOR LATER!

KNOCK, KNOCK.
WHO'S THERE?
HOWARD.
HOWARD WHO?
HOWARD YOU LIKE TO BE KNOCKING ON DOORS ALL DAY?

KNOCK, KNOCK.
WHO'S THERE?
BUTTER.
BUTTER WHO?
BUTTER LET ME IN OR I'LL MELT!

KNOCK KNOCK.
WHO'S THERE?
NANA.
NANA WHO?
NANA YOUR BUSINESS!

KNOCK, KNOCK.
WHO'S THERE?
CAT.
CAT WHO?
CAT YOU LATER, I'M PURRR-TTY BUSY!

KNOCK KNOCK.
WHO'S THERE?
BROKEN PENCIL.
BROKEN PENCIL WHO?
NEVER MIND, IT'S POINTLESS.

KNOCK KNOCK.
WHO'S THERE?
ATCH.
ATCH WHO?
BLESS YOU!

KNOCK KNOCK.
WHO'S THERE?
OWLS SAY.
OWLS SAY WHO?
YES, THEY DO!

KNOCK, KNOCK.
WHO'S THERE?
CEREAL.
CEREAL WHO?
CEREAL-OUSLY, YOU DON'T RECOGNIZE ME?

KNOCK, KNOCK.
WHO'S THERE?
HARRY.
HARRY WHO?
HARRY UP AND ANSWER THE DOOR!

KNOCK, KNOCK.
WHO'S THERE?
SPELL.
SPELL WHO?
W-H-O, THAT'S HOW YOU SPELL WHO!

KNOCK, KNOCK.
WHO'S THERE?
BEAR.
BEAR WHO?
BEAR WITH ME WHILE I THINK OF ANOTHER JOKE!

KNOCK KNOCK.
WHO'S THERE?
ICE CREAM.
ICE CREAM WHO?
ICE CREAM EVERY TIME I SEE
A SPIDER!

KNOCK, KNOCK.
WHO'S THERE?
EUROPE.
EUROPE WHO?
NO, YOU'RE A POO!

KNOCK, KNOCK.
WHO'S THERE?
POLICE
POLICE WHO?
POLICE OPEN THE DOOR, IT'S
COLD OUTSIDE!

KNOCK KNOCK.
WHO'S THERE?
DONUT.
DONUT WHO?
DONUT FORGET TO LAUGH AT THESE JOKES!

KNOCK, KNOCK.
WHO'S THERE?
PEAS.
PEAS WHO?
PEAS LET ME IN!

KNOCK, KNOCK.
WHO'S THERE?
LETTUCE.
LETTUCE WHO?
LETTUCE HAVE PIZZA FOR DINNER!

KNOCK KNOCK.
WHO'S THERE?
ICY.
ICY WHO?
ICY YOU HIDING BEHIND THE DOOR!

RIDDLE ME THIS...

I'M FULL OF HOLES BUT STILL HOLD WATER. WHAT AM I?

A sponge!

THE MORE YOU USE ME, THE SMALLER I GET. WHAT AM I?

A pencil!

I HAVE EARS BUT CAN'T HEAR. I GROW IN A FIELD. WHAT AM I?

Corn!

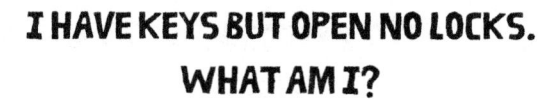

I HAVE KEYS BUT OPEN NO LOCKS. WHAT AM I?

A piano!

I CAN BE CRACKED, MADE, TOLD, AND PLAYED. WHAT AM I?

A joke!

I HAVE HANDS BUT CAN'T CLAP. WHAT AM I?

A clock!

THE MORE YOU TAKE FROM ME, THE BIGGER I GET. WHAT AM I?

A hole!

I START OUT TALL, BUT THE OLDER I GET, THE SHORTER I BECOME. WHAT AM I?

A candle!

I CAN HOLD LOTS OF FOOD AND DRINK YET I CANNOT EAT OR DRINK ANYTHING, WHAT AM I?

A fridge!

WHAT CAN YOU HOLD WITHOUT TOUCHING IT?

Your breath!

YOU CAN SEE ME IN WATER SOMETIMES BUT I NEVER GET WET, WHAT AM I?

A reflection!

I TRAVEL MANY MILES, YET NEVER MOVE, WHAT AM I?

A motorway!

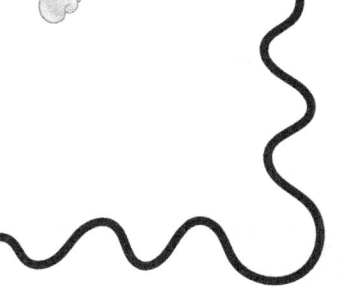

I CAN TRAVEL THROUGH GLASS, WITHOUT BREAKING IT. WHAT AM I?

Light!

WHAT HAS THIRTEEN HEARTS BUT IS NOT ALIVE?

A pack of playing cards!

WHAT HAS TO BE BROKEN BEFORE YOU CAN USE IT?

An egg!

WHAT GOES UP BUT NEVER COMES DOWN?

Your age!

WHAT CAN RUN BUT NEVER WALKS, HAS A BED BUT NEVER SLEEPS, AND HAS A MOUTH BUT NEVER TALKS?

A river!

WHAT HAS A HEAD AND A TAIL, BUT NO BODY?

A coin!

WHAT HAS FOUR LEGS, TWO ARMS BUT NO HEAD?

An armchair!

WHAT BELONGS TO YOU BUT IS USED MORE BY OTHERS?

Your name!

FORWARD I AM HEAVY, BUT BACKWARD I'M NOT. WHAT AM I?

The word "ton"!

THE MORE OF ME YOU TAKE, THE MORE YOU LEAVE BEHIND. WHAT AM I?

Footsteps!

WHAT GETS WETTER THE MORE IT DRIES?

A towel!

WHAT BEGINS WITH AN 'E', ENDS IN AN 'E', HAS AN 'E' IN THE MIDDLE, BUT HAS ONLY ONE LETTER?

An envelope!

I'M NOT ALIVE BUT I HAVE FIVE FINGERS, WHAT AM I?

A glove!

WHAT GOES UP AS RAIN COMES DOWN?

An umbrella!

WHAT KIND OF ROOM HAS NO DOORS OR WINDOWS?

A mushroom!

WHAT IS AT THE END OF THE RAINBOW?

The letter 'w'!

WHAT HAS A NECK BUT NO HEAD?
A bottle!

I AM NOT ALIVE, BUT I CAN GROW. I DON'T HAVE LUNGS, BUT I NEED AIR. I DON'T HAVE A MOUTH, BUT WATER KILLS ME. WHAT AM I?
Fire!

WHAT CAN TRAVEL AROUND THE WORLD WHILE STAYING IN THE SAME CORNER?
A postage stamp!

WHAT CAN RUN BUT CANNOT WALK?
Water!

THE MORE YOU HAVE OF ME, THE LESS YOU SEE. WHAT AM I?

Darkness!

I'M LIGHT AS A FEATHER, YET THE STRONGEST PERSON CAN'T HOLD ME FOR VERY LONG. WHAT AM I?

Your breath!

WHAT HAS MANY TEETH BUT CAN'T BITE?

A comb!

WHAT FLIES, HAS A NOSE, BUT CANNOT SMELL?

An aeroplane!

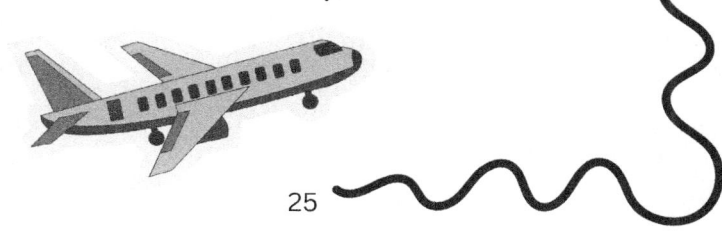

GAGS AND GIGGLES.....

WHAT DID ONE PLATE SAY TO THE OTHER PLATE?

Lunch is on me!

WHY DO DUCKS MAKE GREAT DETECTIVES?

Because they always quack the case!

WHY WERE PEOPLE CLAPPING FOR THE CEILING?

They were ceiling fans!

WHY DID THE BANANA GO TO THE DOCTOR?

Because it wasn't peeling well!

WHY DID THE GOLFER BRING TWO PAIRS OF PANTS?

In case he got a hole in one!

WHAT IS A ROBOT'S FAVOURITE SNACK?

Computer chips!

WHAT DO YOU CALL AN ALLIGATOR IN A VEST?

An investigator!

WHAT DO YOU CALL A MONKEY FLOATING IN THE SKY?

A hot air baboon!

WHY DONT CRABS SHARE THEIR FOOD WITH OTHERS?

Because they are shelfish!

WHY WAS THE TRAFFIC LIGHT LATE FOR HIS DATE?

Because it took him too long to change!

WHAT DO YOU CALL A SLEEPING BULL?

A bulldozer!

WHAT DO YOU CALL A DEER WITH NO EYES?

No eye deer!

WHAT DO YOU CALL A DEER WITH NO EYES AND NO LEGS?

Still no eye deer!

WHAT DO YOU CALL A PIG THAT KNOWS KARATE?

a pork chop!

WHY CAN'T YOU TRUST STAIRS?

Because they're always up to something!

WHAT DO YOU GET WHEN YOU CROSS A FISH AND AN ELEPHANT?

Swimming trunks!

WHAT KIND OF MUSIC DO MUMMIES LISTEN TO?

Wrap music!

WHY DO MATH BOOKS LOOK SO SAD?

Because they have too many problems!

WHAT KIND OF KEY OPENS A BANANA?

A monkey!

WHAT'S THE SMARTEST INSECT?

A spelling bee!

HOW DOES A SCIENTIST FRESHEN HER BREATH?

With experi-mints!

WHY DID THE COOKIE GO TO THE DOCTOR?

Because it felt crummy!

WHAT DID THE PICTURE DO TO END UP IN JAIL?

Nothing, he was framed!

WHAT'S A PIRATE'S FAVOURITE SUBJECT?
Arrrrt!

HOW DO YOU MAKE A TISSUE DANCE?
Put a little boogie in it!

WHAT'S A TORNADO'S FAVOURITE GAME?
Twister!

WHY DID THE TEACHER WEAR SUNGLASSES?
Because her students were so bright!

HOW DO COWS DO MATH?
They use a cow-culator!

WHAT'S ORANGE AND SOUNDS LIKE A PARROT?
A carrot!

WHY CAN'T ELSA HAVE A BALLOON?
Because she'll let it gooo!

WHAT DO YOU CALL A DINOSAUR THAT CRASHES CARS?
Tyrannosaurus wrecks!

WHAT DID THE OCEAN SAY TO THE BEACH?

Nothing, it just waved!

WHY DID THE COW GO TO SPACE?

To see the moooon!

WHAT DO YOU CALL A TRAIN FULL OF BUBBLE GUM?

A chew-chew train!

WHEN IS THE BEST TIME TO VISIT A DENTIST?

Tooth-hurty!

WHY DID THE CHICKEN CROSS THE ROAD?

Because it seemed like an egg-cellent idea!

WHY DID THE DUCK CROSS THE ROAD?

Because it was the chickens day off!

WHY DID THE BUBBLEGUM CROSS THE ROAD?

Because it was stuck to the chicken's foot!

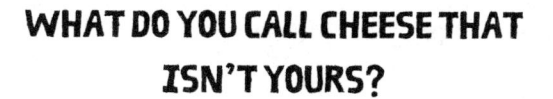

WHAT DO YOU CALL CHEESE THAT ISN'T YOURS?

Nacho cheese!

WHY DID THE APPLE STOP IN THE MIDDLE OF THE ROAD?

Because it ran out of juice!

WHAT'S A GHOST'S FAVOURITE DESSERT?

Boo-berry pie!

WHY DID THE TOMATO BLUSH?

Because it saw the salad dressing!

WHY DON'T EGGS TELL JOKES?

Because they might crack up!

WHAT DO YOU CALL A RABBIT WHO TELLS GOOD JOKES?

A funny bunny!

WHICH ANIMAL SHOULD YOU NEVER PLAY GAMES WITH?

A cheetah!

HOW DO BEES BRUSH THEIR HAIR?

With a honeycomb!

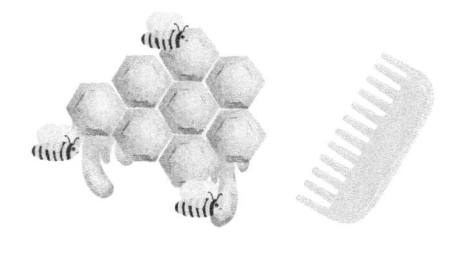

WHAT TIME DO DUCKS WAKE UP?

At the quack of dawn!

HOW DO CHICKENS STAY FIT?

They eggs-ercise!

WHY WAS THE BROOM LATE?

It over swept!

WHAT DID THE JANITOR SHOUT WHEN HE JUMPED OUT OF THE CLOSET?

Supplies!

WHAT DID THE GRAPE DO WHEN IT GOT STEPPED ON?

It let out a little wine!

WHAT WOBBLES AND FLIES?

A jellycopter!

WHAT DO YOU GET IF YOU CROSS A VAMPIRE WITH A SNOWMAN?

Frostbite!

WHY DID THE COMPUTER GO TO THE DOCTOR?

Because it had a virus!

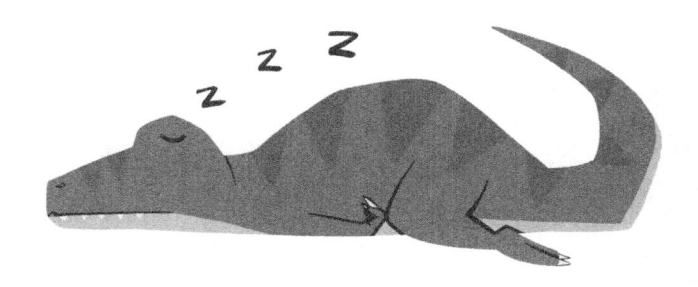

WHAT DO YOU CALL A SLEEPING DINOSAUR?

A dino-snore!

WHAT DO ASTRONAUTS LIKE TO DRINK?

Gravi-Tea!

HOW DO YOU MAKE AN OCTOPUS LAUGH?

With ten-tickles!

WHY ARE FISH SO SMART?

Because they live in schools!

HA HA HA HA

WHAT'S AN AVOCADO'S FAVOURITE KIND OF MUSIC?

Guac 'n' roll!

WHAT DID THE CALCULATOR SAY TO THE MATH STUDENT?

You can count on me!

WHAT IS A FROGS FAVOURITE DRINK?

A croak-a-cola!

WHAT DID ONE EYE SAY TO THE OTHER EYE?

Between you and me, there's something that smells!

WHERE IS A COW'S FAVOURITE PLACE TO GO?

The mooooovies!

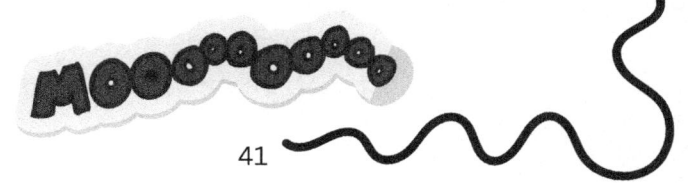

WHERE DO SHEEP GO TO GET THEIR HAIR CUT?

The baa-baa shop!

WHY ARE GHOSTS SUCH BAD LIARS?

Because you can see right through them!

WHY DID THE DOG SIT IN THE SHADE?

Because he didn't want to be a hot dog!

WHY DO FISH LIVE IN SALTWATER?

Because pepper makes them sneeze!

WHAT LIES AT THE BOTTOM OF THE SEA AND WORRIES?

A nervous wreck!

WHAT DO YOU GET IF YOU CROSS A COW WITH A TORNADO?

An udder disaster!

WHY DID THE NINJA GO TO THE DOCTOR?

He had kung-flu!

WHAT DO YOU GET IF YOU CROSS A KITTEN WITH A GHOST?

A scaredy cat!

WHAT DO YOU GET IF YOU CROSS A COW AND A LAWN MOWER?

A lawn-moooer!

WHAT DID THE POLICEMAN SAY TO HIS TUMMY?

Freeze...you are under a vest!

IF YOU HAVE 8 BANANAS IN ONE HAND AND 10 APPLES IN THE OTHER, WHAT DO YOU HAVE?

Really big hands!

WHAT DO YOU GET IF YOU CROSS A SNAKE WITH A BUILDER?

A boa-constructor!

WHAT KIND OF FOOD DOES A SPRINTER EAT?

Fast food!

WHERE DO PEOPLE GO WHEN THEY HAVE TWO BROKEN LEGS?

Nowhere!

WHY CAN'T YOU TRUST AN ATOM?

Because they make up everything!

WHY WAS NUMBER SIX AFRAID OF NUMBER SEVEN?

Because seven eight nine!

WHY CAN'T YOU PLAY A TRICK ON A SNAKE?

Because you can't pull his leg!

HOW DO BEES GET TO SCHOOL?
By school buzz!

WHY DID THE STUDENT EAT HIS HOMEWORK?
Because the teacher said it was a piece of cake!

WHAT DO YOU CALL A FAKE NOODLE?
An impasta!

WHY DIDN'T THE FROG PARK HIS CAR ON THE STREET?
He didn't want to get toad!

WHAT DO YOU GET WHEN YOU CROSS A SHEEP AND A KANGAROO?

A woolly jumper!

WHY DID THE TIGER SPIT OUT THE CLOWN?

He tasted funny!

WHAT'S A SKELETON'S LEAST FAVOURITE ROOM?

The living room!

WHAT'S A SNAKE'S FAVOURITE SUBJECT IN SCHOOL?

Hiss-story!

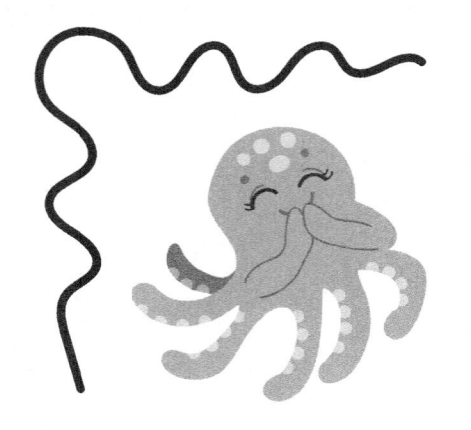

WHY DID THE OCTOPUS BLUSH?

Because the sea weed!

WHY DO PENCILS NEVER GET LOST?

Because they always draw attention!

WHAT DID ONE TOILET SAY TO THE OTHER?

You look a little flushed!

WHAT HAS SIX EYES BUT CANNOT SEE?

Three blind mice!

WHY DID THE SKELETON GO TO THE PARTY ALONE?

Because he had no body to go with!

WHAT DID THE DUCK SAY WHEN IT BOUGHT LIPSTICK?

Put it on my bill!

WHAT DO DUCKS LOVE TO EAT WITH CHEESE?

Quakers!

WHAT DO YOU CALL A THREE LEGGED DONKEY?

Wonkey!

WHICH RUNS FASTER, HOT OR COLD?

Hot.. because anyone can catch a cold!

WHY ARE NINJA FARTS SO DANGEROUS?

They are silent but deadly!

WHAT DO YOU CALL A FAIRY WHO WON'T WASH?

Stinker-bell!

WHAT'S A PIRATE'S FAVOURITE INSTRUMENT?

The guitarrrrrrr!

WHAT KIND OF SHOES DO SPIES WEAR?

Sneakers!

WHAT KIND OF PARTIES DO PENGUINS LIKE TO ATTEND?

Snow-balls!

WHAT DID THE PAINTER SAY TO THE WALL?

Don't worry, I've got you covered!

WHAT DO YOU CALL A DINOSAUR WITH NO EYES?

Do-you-think-he-saurus!

HOW DOES AN ASTRONAUT STOP A BABY FROM CRYING?

Rocket to sleep!

WHAT SEASON DO YOU PLAY ON A TRAMPOLINE?

Spring time!

WHAT DOES A DUCK LIKE TO WATCH ON TV?

The feather forecast!

WHAT DID ONE WALL SAY TO THE OTHER WALL?

I'll meet you at the corner!

HOW DID THE VET TREAT THE PIG WITH A RASH?

Easy, he just needed a little oinkment!

WHY DID THE TEDDY BEAR SAY NO TO DESSERT?

Because he was stuffed!

WHAT DO YOU CALL A FISH WITHOUT EYES?
Fsh!

HOW DO YOU ORGANISE A SPACE PARTY?
You planet!

WHY DID THE BOY TAKE TOILET ROLL TO THE PARTY?
Because he was a party pooper!

HOW DO YOU MAKE A LEMON DROP?
Just let it fall!

HOW DO ASTRONAUTS DRINK THEIR TEA?
From flying saucers!

WHAT DID ONE SNOWMAN SAY TO THE OTHER SNOWMAN?

"Do you smell carrots?"

WHAT DO YOU GET WHEN YOU CROSS A VAMPIRE WITH A DUCK?

Count Quackula!

WHAT DO YOU CALL A FISH THAT WEARS A BOWTIE?

Sofishticated!

WHY WAS THE LIBRARY SO TALL?

Because it had so many stories!

HOW DOES THE MOON CUT HIS HAIR?
Eclipse it!

WHAT DO YOU CALL A TRANSFORMER BUNNY?
Hop-timus Prime!

WHY DID THE CHOCOLATE GO TO SCHOOL?
Because he wanted to be a smartie!

WHAT'S A CAT'S FAVOURITE COLOUR?
Purrr-ple!

WHAT MEDICINE DO YOU USE TO TREAT A SICK ANT?

Ant-i-biotics!

WHAT IS BROWN AND STICKY?

A stick!

WHY DID THE LITTLE GIRL PUT SUGAR UNDER HER PILLOW?

So she could have sweet dreams!

WHAT DOES A CLOUD WEAR TO SCHOOL?

Thunderwear!

WHAT KIND OF CANDY DO YOU EAT ON THE PLAYGROUND?

Recess pieces!

WHAT'S A VAMPIRE'S FAVOURITE FRUIT?

A blood orange!

WHAT DID THE VOLCANO SAY TO THE OTHER VOLCANO?

I lava you!

WHERE DO ASTRONAUTS KEEP THEIR SANDWICHES?

In their launch box!

WHY DID THE OWL GET AN AWARD?

Because he was owl-standing!

WHAT'S A SKELETON'S FAVOURITE INSTRUMENT?

A trom-bone!

WHAT DO YOU CALL A SHEEP THAT KNOWS KARATE?

A lamb-chop!

WHAT DO YOU CALL A SHEEP COVERED IN CHOCOLATE?

A Candy baa!

HOW DO YOU KNOW WHEN THE MOON HAS HAD ENOUGH TO EAT?

When it's full!

WHAT KIND OF BUTTON WON'T UNBUTTON?

A bellybutton!

LOL

WHY DON'T TURKEYS GET INVITED TO DINNER PARTIES?

Because of their fowl language!

WHY DID THE COW GO TO MUSIC CLASS?

To improve it's moo-sical skills!

WHAT DO YOU CALL A HORSE THAT LIVES NEXT DOOR?

Your neigh-bor!

WHY DID THE FISH BLUSH?

Because it saw the ocean's bottom!

WHY WAS THE CAT SITTING ON THE COMPUTER?

It wanted to keep an eye on the mouse!

HOW DO COWS STAY UP TO DATE?

They read the moo-s paper!

WHAT DO YOU CALL TWO BIRDS IN LOVE?

Tweethearts!

WHAT DID THE FROG ORDER AT THE FAST-FOOD RESTAURANT?

French flies and a diet croak!

WHY DON'T KOALAS COUNT AS BEARS?

Because they don't have the koalafications!

WHY ARE SPIDERS SO SMART?

Because they spend a lot of time on the web!

WHAT DO YOU CALL A SNAIL ON A SHIP?

A snailer!

WHAT DID ONE ELEVATOR SAY TO THE OTHER ELEVATOR?

I think I'm coming down with something!

WHY DID THE BANANA GO OUT WITH THE PRUNE?

Because it couldn't find a date!

WHAT DO PLANETS LIKE TO READ?

Comet books!

WHAT DID THE MAGICIAN SAY AFTER HIS RABBIT VANISHED?

Hare today, gone tomorrow!

HOW DO YOU KNOW WHEN A CLOWN HAS FARTED?

It smells funny!

WHAT DID THE SOCK SAY TO THE FOOT?

You're toe-tally awesome!

WHY DID THE ERASER BREAK UP WITH THE PENCIL?

Because it made too many mistakes!

WHY DID THE YOGURT GO TO THE ART EXHIBIT?

Because it was cultured!

HAHAHA

WHAT DO YOU CALL A CAMEL WITH NO HUMPS?

Humphrey!

WHY DID THE MAGICIAN FAIL MATH CLASS?

Because he kept pulling numbers out of his hat!

WHY SHOULD YOU NEVER FART IN AN ELEVATOR?

Because it's wrong on so many levels!

WHAT DO YOU CALL A BEAR WHO'S STUCK IN THE RAIN?

A drizzly bear!

WHAT DO YOU CALL A COW THAT TELLS JOKES?

A laughing stock!

WHAT DID ONE SHOE SAY TO THE OTHER?

We make a great pair!

WHAT DO YOU CALL A DINOSAUR FART?

A blast from the past!

AT SCHOOL, WHERE DO FROGS KEEP THEIR COATS?

In the croakroom!

WHAT DID THE TREE SAY TO THE WIND?

Go away and leaf me alone!

HOW DID A BARBER WIN THE 'LONG RUN' RACE?

Easy, he knew all the short cuts!

WHAT DID THE BEAVER SAY TO THE TREE?

Its been nice gnawing you!

WHAT DO YOU CALL A PIG THAT PAINTS?

Pablo Pigcasso!

WHAT'S A VAMPIRE'S FAVOURITE SPORT?

Bat-minton!

DOCTOR DOCTOR......

DOCTOR, DOCTOR! I SWALLOWED A ROLL OF FILM!

Let's hope nothing develops!

DOCTOR, DOCTOR, I KEEP THINKING I'M A BELL!

Well, take these and if they don't work—give me a ring!

DOCTOR, DOCTOR, I THINK I'M A DOG!

Lie down on the couch.
I CAN'T—I'M NOT ALLOWED ON THE FURNITURE!

DOCTOR, DOCTOR, PEOPLE KEEP IGNORING ME!

Next!

DOCTOR, DOCTOR, I FEEL LIKE A DECK OF CARDS!

I'll deal with you later!

DOCTOR, DOCTOR, I FEEL LIKE A PAIR OF CURTAINS!

Just pull yourself together!

DOCTOR, DOCTOR, CAN YOU GIVE ME SOMETHING FOR MY WIND?

Yes, have a kite!

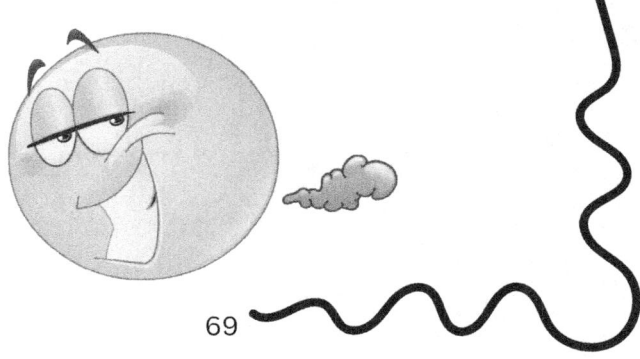

DOCTOR, DOCTOR, I KEEP SEEING DOUBLE!

Take a seat.
WHICH ONE?

DOCTOR, DOCTOR, I STOOD ON A PEICE OF LEGO!

Try to block out the pain!

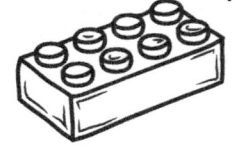

DOCTOR, DOCTOR, I FEEL LIKE A SPOON!

Sit still and don't stir!

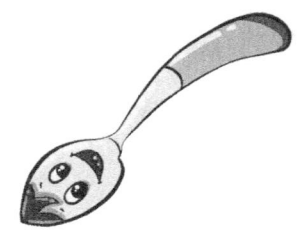

DOCTOR, DOCTOR, I'M SHRINKING!

You'll just have to be a little patient!

DOCTOR, DOCTOR, I FEEL LIKE A CHICKEN!

How long has this been going on?
EVER SINCE I CAME OUT OF MY SHELL!

DOCTOR, DOCTOR, I'VE BROKEN MY ARM IN SEVERAL PLACES!

Well, don't go to those places!

DOCTOR, DOCTOR, EVERYONE THINKS I AM A LIAR!

Well I cannot believe that!

DOCTOR, DOCTOR, I CAN'T HELP IT BUT I KEEP STEALING THINGS!

Have you taken anything for it?

DOCTOR, DOCTOR, I KEEP SEEING SPOTS IN FRONT OF MY EYES!

Have you seen an optician?
NO, JUST SPOTS!

HAHA!

DOCTOR, DOCTOR, I THINK I'M A BEE!

Buzz off — I'm busy!

DOCTOR, DOCTOR, I CAN'T GET TO SLEEP!

Lie on the edge of the bed — you'll soon drop off!

EGGS-CELLENT EASTER JOKES....

WHY DID THE EASTER EGG HIDE?

It was a little chicken!

WHAT HAPPENED TO THE EASTER BUNNY WHEN HE MISBEHAVED AT SCHOOL?

He got egg-spelled!

WHY DID THE CHICKEN JOIN A BAND?

Because it had the drumsticks!

WHAT DO YOU CALL A RABBIT WITH FLEAS?

Bugs Bunny!

WHAT DO YOU GET WHEN YOU POUR HOT WATER DOWN A RABBIT HOLE?

Hot cross bunnies!

WHY DON'T RABBITS EVER GET HOT IN THE SUMMER?

Because they have hare-conditioning!

WHY WAS THE EASTER BUNNY SO GRUMPY?

He was having a bad hare day!

WHY WAS THE EASTER BUNNY HIRED FOR THE JOB?

He had the most eggs-perience!

WHAT DO YOU CALL A VERY TIRED EASTER EGG?

Eggs-hausted!

WHAT DO YOU CALL AN EGG THAT PLAYS TRICKS?

A practical yoker!

HOW CAN YOU TELL WHICH RABBITS ARE OLD?

Look for the grey hares!

WHAT KIND OF MUSIC DO EASTER BUNNIES LISTEN TO?

Hip-hop!

WHY DOES THE EASTER BUNNY HAVE SUCH GOOD SKIN?

he eggs-foliates!

WHY DON'T YOU SEE DINOSAURS AT EASTER?

Because they are eggs-tinct!

WHAT DO YOU CALL AN EASTER EGG FROM OUTER SPACE?

An egg-straterrestrial!

HALLOWEEN HOWLERS...

WHAT DO YOU CALL A WITCH WHO LIVES AT THE BEACH?

A sand-witch!

WHY DON'T MONSTERS EAT CLOWNS?

They taste funny!

WHAT'S A GHOST'S FAVOURITE EXERCISE?

Dead lifts!

WHY ARE GRAVEYARDS SO NOISY?
Because of all the coffin!

WHY DON'T MUMMIES TAKE VACATIONS?
They're afraid they'll unwind!

HOW DO MONSTERS LIKE THEIR EGGS?
Terror-fried!

WHERE DO BABY GHOSTS GO DURING THE DAY?
Dayscare!

WHAT DOES A WITCH USE TO KEEP HER HAIR IN PLACE?
Scare spray!

WHY DID THE ZOMBIE SKIP SCHOOL?

He felt rotten!

WHERE WILL YOU FIND ZOMBIES SWIMMING?

In the dead sea!

WHY DON'T GHOSTS LIKE RAIN?

It dampens their spirits!

WHAT'S A GHOST'S FAVOURITE RIDE AT THE FAIR?

The roller-ghoster!

WHAT DO YOU CALL A SKELETON CLEANER?

The grim sweeper!

WHAT KIND OF DOG DOES DRACULA HAVE?
A bloodhound!

WHY DO GHOSTS LIKE TO RIDE IN ELEVATORS?
It lifts their spirits!

WHAT GAME DO LITTLE GHOSTS LOVE TO PLAY?
Hide and shriek!

WHAT DO YOU CALL TWO WITCHES WHO LIVE TOGETHER?
Broommates!

CHRISTMAS CRACKERS...

WHY WAS THE SNOWMAN LOOKING THROUGH A BAG OF CARROTS?

He was picking his nose!

WHAT DO REINDEER HANG ON THEIR CHRISTMAS TREES?

Horn-aments!

WHAT DO YOU CALL SANTA WHEN HE TAKES A BREAK?

Santa Pause!

HOW DO SNOWMEN GET AROUND?

By-icicle!

WHAT DO SNOWMEN EAT FOR BREAKFAST?

Frosted flakes!

WHAT MAKE OF CAR DO ELVES DRIVE?

Toy-otas!

WHAT DO YOU CALL A RICH ELF?

Welfy!

WHY DON'T YOU EVER SEE SANTA IN THE HOSPITAL?

He has private elf care!

HOW DO ELVES KEEP THEIR HANDS SO CLEAN?

They use plenty of Santa-tizer!

WHAT DO YOU CALL SANTA'S RUDEST REINDEER?

Rude-olph!

WHAT DID RUDOLPH SAY TO THE ELF WHEN FLYING FAST?

Hold on for deer life!

WHAT KIND OF MONEY DO ELVES USE?

Jingle bills!

WHAT'S AN ELF'S FAVOURITE SPORT?

North Pole vaulting!

WHAT IS AN ELF'S FAVOURITE TYPE OF PHOTO?

Elfies! (especially when using their elfie stick)

WHAT DO YOU GET WHEN YOU CROSS A BELL WITH A SKUNK?

Jingle smells!

WHERE DO ELVES GO TO VOTE?

The north poll!

WHAT KIND OF KEY DO YOU NEED FOR A NATIVITY PLAY?

A don-key!

WHAT DO YOU CALL A CAT ON THE BEACH DURING CHRISTMAS?

Sandy Claws!

WHAT DO YOU GET IF YOU EAT CHRISTMAS DECORATIONS?

Tinselitis!

WHAT DO YOU CALL A SNOWMAN IN SUMMER?

A puddle!

WHY DID SANTA NEED TO WEAR A HARD HAT IN HIS TOY FACTORY?

Because of elf and safety!

WHY DID THE ELF GO TO SCHOOL?

To learn the elf-abet!

WHAT DO YOU GET IF YOU CROSS AN ELF WITH A DUCK?

A Christmas quacker!

WHAT DO YOU CALL AN ELF THAT WONT SHARE?

Elfish!

ULTIMATE TONGUE TWISTER CHALLENGE...

LETS WARM UP WITH THE FIRST BATCH...

SIX SLIPPERY SNAILS SLID SLOWLY SEAWARD.

PETER PIPER PICKED A PECK OF PICKLED PEPPERS.

COOKS COOK CUPCAKES QUICKLY.

THE SHORT SOLDIER SHOOTS STRAIGHT

SHE SELLS SEA SHELLS ON THE SEA SHORE.

LETS MOVE TO THE MORE ADVANCED LEVEL...

HE THREW THREE FREE THROWS.

LOL

FRED FED TED BREAD AND TED FED FRED BREAD.

I SLIT THE SHEET, THE SHEET I SLIT, AND ON THE SLITTED SHEET I SIT.

I SAW SUSIE SITTING IN A SHOE SHINE SHOP...

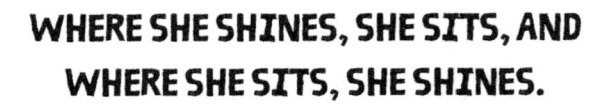

WHERE SHE SHINES, SHE SITS, AND WHERE SHE SITS, SHE SHINES.

NOW FOR THE ULTIMATE CHALLENGE...

YOU HAVE TO SAY THESE AS FAST AS YOU CAN...

MISSION IMPOSSIBLE

RED LORRY, YELLOW LORRY (X5).

BLUE GLUE GUN, GREEN GLUE GUN (X5).

SHE SEES CHEESE (X5).

FRESHLY FRIED FLYING FISH (X5).

TOY BOAT (X5).

UNIQUE NEW YORK (X5).

Well, that's it! Thanks for laughing along! I hope you had a giggle reading.. **Probably The Best Joke Book In The World! For Kids.**

If you enjoyed these silly, crazy jokes, then guess what? The fun doesn't stop here! Check out my other books:

Did You Know? 100 Crazy Facts For Kids About Animals

and

Did You Know? 100 Crazy Facts For Kids About Space

These books are packed with weird, wacky, and totally true facts that will blow your mind!

Available to purchase on Amazon

Printed in Dunstable, United Kingdom